DREAMLANDS

Aigen

I0158617

ISBN: 978-1-913642-44-0

Book designed by Aaron Kent

Edited by Aaron Kent

Broken Sleep Books (2021), Talgarreg, Wales

Contents

Dreamlands

Razielle Aigen

Imprint

"Tu ne sais ni où tu vas ni pourquoi tu vas ; entre
partout, réponds à tout . . ."
   — Arthur Rimbaud, Mauvais sang, Une saison en enfer

"You do not know where you are going, nor
why you are going; enter anywhere, reply to anything."
   — Arthur Rimbaud, "Bad Blood," A Season in Hell

Enter anywhere. Be diaphanous.
Make soft your shape.
Cat. Cow. Cobbler. Shell.
Let the softness, the inkiness of you
settle in in the intaglio. Seep
like walnut oil into carved coper
ridges of line and form.
Leave an impression.
Leave an imprint,
a mark of your body.
Be heavy enough.
Be here enough. Decide
on something and then make it
soft, translucent.

Become a feather and float.
Become a winter moon and shimmer.
Become iridescent as amaranth.
Give a blood curdling balk — go ahead, wake them!

Now imagine sunlight glittering on the snow.
Now imagine sunlight dizzily drinking an open field.
Now imagine a wooded creek encircled by a thousand
shapes of death, shades
of the lily-livered that lay dormant within us, now departed
so that we may recoup,
so that we may regain our ruddiness and footholds
in rebirth.

Learning
to bear the radiance of it all.
Every swollen ego and effective trust.
Every malevolent gold-digger and virgin Mary Magdalene.
Every last revolver and open heart.

And I wonder, is it possible?
Can rage be distilled enough to be abandoned?
Just checking,
because it's pisces season and the light of the crepuscule is mutable.
These signs are minuscule, but please, read them carefully.
Hold on to the banisters.
Something is shifting.

We've Been Dreaming This for Eons

In search of clarity
a definitive all caps nope is preferable
to the conceptual form of you
the you that goes to bed as a one
and then wakes up more as a zero
that you, but in reverse
more absence than presence

In your dreams you're you
but the B side

Encoded in a forest
there's an embedded lake
sometimes
you bring me to the edge and then
walk away

I fall in

Like rain that comes just before disappearing
into the woods, it's case by case
Every forest is its own thing
Every forest does its own thinking
sometimes splitting its trees
like wishbones or tuning forks

It feels like the splitting is an ok thing
because we have the feeling that it is
and then, when we don't
it isn't

Overnight, encased by nightfall
the trees and lake bear witness
to an ancient dream and a mass grave

I am only one mirror, you say, *and the middle of the lake is a different point of view.*

This, I say, *is what happens when you don't pay attention to your unconscious.*

When you speak you have something
that resembles a lisp but isn't
an impediment
something like knotted sinew webbing
laced across the oracular caverns
of your history

It sometimes catches dreams

Filtering the inverse of necessity
you find yourself in nothing but a sometimes
mirrored lake reflecting
trees and light

I come back to bed in the mornings to dream in your dreams
Sometimes I'm still dreaming you and you are
sometimes still dreaming me

but in reverse

Light. Lake. Trees. Memory. Rain.

I am a lake in the middle of a forest doing my own thing, thinking
about your mirrored presence

then, like light
I will have disappeared in the trees

Low-key

you're low-key having synesthesia
    as you imagine how thinking would taste.
        a bit bitter, probably. a metallic residue of aluminum

on your tongue as your mind is illumined
    by thoughts of what it might be like
        to turn down the volume on mother

and not think so generic. like bauxite,
    the raw material of your molecular structure
        is akin to the composition of your bare life,

boxed into the life form that you are, limited
    only by the movements of your mind at this very moment.
        like, I am your left eye and the only one left here.

like, I am your your ugliness
    when you let your true colours show.
        glyphs rising and falling, a rivering

of thinking that poisons otherwise potable pathways.
    you go stand over there and look out the window
        and say how nice it would be if we could hear nature,

not the wind and the animals, but something else,
something more primal.

you're low-key spewing everything
    that bothers you, not convincing anyone
        that you're not a lapsed vegetarian,
            that veganism is not a hobby.

you're low-key self-diagnosing
    a low glow disorder. paleontologists
        will later mistakenly call this an aptitude

for sonnets, saying it was good to express
    healthy aggression by biting into a Granny Smith,
        piercing waxy chartreuse skin with central
            and lateral incisors,

teeth sink into pith as a means
    of displacing and dissipating rage — if only!
        an undoing of lifetimes.

you're low-key using poetry as a user
    friendly platform for raising consciousness,
        beginning with your own excavation of thought,

dismantling toxic relations, unskillful behaviour, and biographical
    wounds. you're thinking *maybe in my next life I'll come back*
        as you, as your deficiencies

are pointed out to you by a loved one,
    making you squirm and gnash your teeth, making you want
        to mash you face into the nearest moss covered geode

rendering you unrecognizable
even to yourself, as if you witnessed your own birth.

for the time being, you're low-key thinking
        about making a sculpture of a head, but leaving out the right ear
                so that you can hear only the left side voices of the unconscious

you're working on perfecting a philosophy
        of moment to moment body awareness,
                perfecting your veaganism, which is neither a religion
                        nor a hobby.

you're banking on leaving flowers of yourself behind
when you go.

There is No Telos

it's been said
there is no telos
& so
would it not be
easier if
we let the leaves
speak for themselves
through the shimmer of
white wine light
cloven
to the negative
space
between
leathered branches

would it not be
easier if
we reinvest our trust
in water
that patient carver
in cahoots with Time
always finding a way
around & through
the hard places
cooling
private sulphuric
infernos
that cause skin to erupt
& nerve endings
to burn

it's been said
there is no telos
& so
the earth's utterance
of fire is directionless

combustive
& yes
to some degree
communicative —

but to what end?

Ode to Hermes

We are thinking to ourselves, just as we arrive
in a deluge, *well that's just great, no raincoats, no umbrellas.*
Proving again that we are water,
proving again that despite all horrors
we are true and beautiful and kind.

Overcoming guru death, surpassing false idols of id
we reestablish healthy boundaries
we dance around the kitchen in socks and underwear to a mix
of guilt and opportunism of holocaust tourism
inadvertently our travels will have lead us here
to see for ourselves what traces remain.
We place stones on Lithuanian forest tombs and mass graves.
We eat french fries doused in paprika and mayonnaise.

Let life grease its own gears. This is just to say
please don't micromanage or use me as baroque leverage
to circumvent the ornate fate of intertwined snakes
or any other gilded amulet of history.
Let's just pretend it's by design god, that I've designed this
shield to shield humankind from itself.
There is always the danger of too much
symbiosis. It is possible, also, I've heard
to suffer from your own beauty
and that painting can serve as catharsis, as memory banks.

What's one more notch in your Borscht belt? The levity
of those far-away Catskills that helped you forget
the warped, waterlogged wooden
homes of the old country with their triangular roofs
and lace curtains that stayed mum, never letting on
that a backyard genocide was going on
within our lifetime. Let's paint an inverted paradise
as a metaphor for betrayal
a guideline on how to invite incantations of Baltic shamans

whose broken Sanskrit, gnarled ginger root knuckles and
withered leather satchels paint you inadvertently

in the form of a red teardrop camouflaged
by landscape, lucid against the backdrop of biodiversity
in the pines, blending you into quiet forests of residual horror.
Everyone is born into a difficult incarnation.

Still, you're watery, rippled and not fully formed.
Still, you swoon. Mystified by the psychic life of trees
and the unconscious, coniferous alterity of your soul, here
again after so very long.

Antediluvian Forest

You can see the old growth forest as a body
the naked November branches, the dendrites
of your neurones
the heavy of oak trunks, the coarseness
of your enormous thighs.
Their roots, your roots. Your underground
rhizomic unconscious, tangled
in the nodes of a karmic thicket.

You can see the body as a temple, primeval
with a diadem of trees beaming on a hilltop
brushing the clouds crowded in
like upside down mountains
illumined tangerine from within, reflected in a pristine
clearwater lake, its source a rushing waterfall
an outpouring, a rent in the hardness
of your petrified rock face.

Dusk. The hour between dog and wolf
in which doubt corrodes the heart
the brilliance of the day
conceding that it can too be beautiful to become
less beautiful, beautiful to grow old. A shift
towards nightfall. The weirdness
of aging. Running, we lie
that we like how it makes us feel
when really we like how it makes us look.
Vibrant, youthful, eternal.

The forest path is soft and supple, forgiving
every breathless heal-toe stride of vanity, absorbing
the shock and anxious mourning of a bird's nest
chest, burrowed in patterns of ancestral grief
home to a fragile, unhatched
speckled egg and a sunken heart

not relatable to anything actual
a deceptive residual depression of deep time
nourished by not doing anything
to decrease its volume or soften its cardiovascular impact.

And maybe there's meaning
in the weirdness. Or maybe it's just weird.

You wake up and wonder. What if
everyone decides in hive-mind collectivity to love
you all at once, despite your compulsive running
despite the tropes of your mind transfigured
by rock knots of inherited guilt and anger and
your congenital personality defects daisy-chained into an aura
around you that makes them say *boy, she's moody!*

On some level, you know
being natural is just as much a contrivance.
On some level, you know
you'll keep running in the forest.

Sweet pea, zucchini, lemon balm & lupine

asters & thistle, clematis & lily, beets
& arugula, lettuce & thyme, oregano, mint
basil, phlox & carrots, radishes, spinach, raspberry
tomatoes & cucumber.

A garden lined with amoral daffodils
uptight crocuses and strewn

with stinking drunk peonies
too bone weary to remove the mascara streaming

down their cheeks, no shame
in their explosive tattered bursts

of hysterical pink anger
and general over-the-top too muchness

all tangles and untameable, wild
and without care

for the mundane burdens of being.
Laissez-faire bonnes vivantes, couldn't care less

that we had just re-emerged
from yet another Mile End winter, only just barely

scraping by under a muted darkness
cast over the hemisphere

in which we hadn't banked
on the hollowness of bones becoming

another person's structural integrity
transplanted and unearthed

amidst a forgiveness radiant and mellow.

In our permacultured heart
of hearts there is always this sense of almost

belonging, though everything about it
feels more like longing

for a reality that we're slowly, only
now reconfiguring ourselves around.

A rusted train yard covered over in white
silence waits for

spring, thawing its way into beginning.
We'll look back at the snow covered tracks

that separated us all winter long
from Little Italy and think to ourselves

how well we kept our balance
between how much everything mattered

and how easy it was to erase.

Intermingled Sibyls

Sibylle says I have one foot
        already in another realm
        but that the rest of me is still here
inside, in something of a threshold

a productive juxtaposition
        the pain of which might be
        something akin to birthing yourself
into existence. She isn't wrong.

She asks, *and what will you do*
        about your name? when I tell her
        you want to blend our biologies
into a hyphenated togetherness that will outlast being.

I say, *I really hadn't thought of it . . .*
        I'm still in the gap time
between
        knowing and seeing.
In a wish to live more, in granular hope, Sybil held

a fistful of sand, and asked Apollo for eternity.
        In another instance, she crafted an omen
        a book of a future underworld disguised
as beauty, and asked for nothing.

I'm thinking of the German word for lightly-falling-snow
        Sibylle enters the kitchen, hands me an accordion-
        folded scrap of paper stitched with a thin white thread
then walks away. I stain it beetroot in the unfolding.

Sibylle's iridescent dulse and violet
      skirts of raw silk are lovely, they rustle when she walks.
      In a dream I think how nice it would be for us to stitch
our hands together in a blanket, taking me with her when
she goes.

I want to ask, *will you watch over me while I sleep?*

A pale yellow-grey sun
      sets behind the tight-knit
      opalescence of clouds looming
low over the fjord.

                                     Snow is whispering from the sky

Dream Borderlands

I am not your Iphigenia
oh father, you

who are not here anymore
to dispense judgement

disapproval or blessing
willy nilly like the wind when she wildly interferes

taking with her what she whirlingly wills, unhinging
doors right from their frames

carrying off to oblivion anything
not sufficiently tied down —

she shows no mercy.
dear you, father

I am not a sonnet but you can
if you must, interpret these dream borderlands

in which your future self is watching you
in your endless sleep

in which you win your war over the wind.
the ruins now seem fitting as a starting place.

k, bye

if the pale morning
moon were still
to faintly linger
with sky-blue sluicing
through her irregular
rice paper surface
as a lasting impression
made in a subjunctive mood
by the night;
then the sky (as a context
for the conditional)
will become paralyzing
contingent on doubt
and the quietude
of a palaeolithic night.

(the time long before
we came to know ourselves)

here
in this pale place
of if
of other
of opacity
admittedly
none of your lobster-coloured geraniums
go unnoticed.
flower by passing flower
you leave no broken hearts.

k, bye you say
and I wonder
how many lifetimes
we'll dream through this
fading facade
of night.

Acknowledgements

With gratitude . . . and heartfelt thanks to my family, friends, and community of writers who have sustained me over the years.

Much appreciation for Canada Council for the Arts for supporting my creative research.

And to the fine journals that published prior permutations of poems found in this collection — many thanks! **Imprint** (previously published as **Banisters**) and **Ode to Hermes** appeared in *There Is The River;* **We've Been Dreaming This for Eons** appeared in *Terse. journal;* **There is No Telos** appeared in *Cypress Journal;* **Antediluvian Forest** appeared in *Deluge;* **Dream Borderlands** appeared in *Ghost City Review;* **Intermingled Sibyls** appeared in *Can We Have Our Ball Back?;* **k, bye** appeared in *Pamenar Press.*

LAY OUT YOUR UNREST